Manifest Li

Hack Reality With Simple Money Magic

If The Secret Worked You'd Already Be Wealthy.

Discover The Mysterious Process That Brings You Anything You Want In Minutes

Michael Ellington

Copyright © 2014 Michael Ellington

All Rights Reserved. This book may not be reproduced, in whole or in part, in any form or by any means electronic or mechanical, including photocopying, recording, or by any information storage retrieval system now known or hereafter invented, without written permission from the publisher, Michael Ellington

What others are saying about Manifest Like The Rich

'Thank you so much for writing such an excellent book. I've read TONS of Law of Attraction books, and now I think I'm going to pack all of them up and store them away somewhere! I don't need anything else. Your book is so precise and so brilliant. Thanks again for such a great book!' - *Sarah M, San Jose, CA*

'I am so grateful I bought your book! I have never had real, fully successful results like this so quickly! I have to thank you again because I have never read anything about the Law Of Attraction or The Secret that works for real! Thank you thank you thank you!' - *Emma H, Washington DC*

CONTENTS

Uncovering The One Process

Beyond The Law of Attraction

The Impossible Becomes Real

Will It Really Work?

Does It Work For Everything?

When Power Comes Easily

Just The Facts

You Don't Need To Believe

The Secret of All Success

The Pattern of Success

How To Stay Successful

The Power of Results

Beyond Positive Thinking

The One Process

Don't Limit Your Dreams

Any Feeling Will Do

Unlocking The One Process

Working With Universal Powers

Making Money

Two Important Questions

What to think about?

More On The Six Principles

Questions and Answers

Seven Secrets For Attracting A Better Life

Getting Results

Uncovering The One Process

There is a secret principle used by the rich, the famous and the powerful. This principle goes way beyond success techniques such as The Law of Attraction, Positive Thinking, Meditation or Visualization. It is the power to attract exactly what you want, unbelievably fast.

Imagine what it's like to see your desires manifesting, just minutes after you apply this principle. It does happen. I once used this technique to make something happen, and within minutes I received a phone call, telling me that my wish had come true.

But you should also know that sometimes it takes years for things to manifest. If you've just taken your first acting lesson, it's going to take years to win that Oscar. This is common sense. I would be a liar if I suggested anything else.

But let's imagine you've taken your first acting lesson and want to audition for your first play, or your first short film. The One Process can get you the role. In this sense, it does make miracles happen. It does work fast.

If you have a goal, The One Process will make every step easier than it would otherwise have been.

Whatever your quest, this power will make everything fall into place at exactly the right time. You'll get the breaks you need and the luck you deserve.

Beyond The Law of Attraction

You've probably read about success techniques and great secrets, used by the wealthy and famous. Most people have heard about The Law of Attraction – the idea being that what you hold in your mind comes into your life. This works for many people.

The information you read in most Law of Attraction books is good, accurate and true, but it isn't the whole story. There must be something in it, though, because it has been used by many famous people, and there are countless reports of success. There are also many failures.

Sadly, many people get excited by The Law of Attraction because they manifest a parking space, or attract a few extra dollars, but then the 'law' seems to stop working. The gurus say you attract everything through your vibration, so you feel guilty that you're not vibrating properly. For the gurus this is a win-win situation. If you get what you want, it's because of The Law. If not, it's your fault for doing it wrong. Thankfully, there is a better way.

The truth is that The Law of Attraction secrets work – sometimes - because they are tapping into a greater power. The problem is that most of the books – even the ones you love so much – treat The Law of Attraction like a religion and refuse to question its teachings. That's why there are so many books trying to explain *The Secret*. If it really worked so easily, everybody would be out there manifesting exactly what they want.

I've even heard people say, "I've been listening to Law of Attraction material for fifteen years, and I really love it, but I'm still poor." Frankly, I don't think that's a good result. I don't want you to spend fifteen years getting rich.

I searched for a secret to success for over three decades. I digested hundreds of books – nearly a thousand, in fact – in an attempt to find the secret to success. None of those books gave me what I needed.

The most popular theories in recent history have all been based on variations of The Law of Attraction or New Thought as it is known. It's been known by other names, and sold and packaged in a hundred different ways, but just about every success guru says that to get what you want you should use the power of your mind.

Thoughts are things, the books told me. If you imagine your desires, with feeling, and then 'let go', your dreams will come true.

But I didn't have much luck with this. After all, how do you 'let go', when you really want something?

A few years ago I met a group of people who used something else. They used The One Process. I was lucky enough to get to know this group well, and after a short time, they revealed the process to me.

I felt like I'd been initiated into a secret society, because they gave me access to a power that made things work out the way I wanted them to, within hours.

The Impossible Becomes Real

If this sounds implausible, that's fine. It sounded implausible to me as well. But I practiced the technique, just for a few months, and it worked.

Within weeks, money was turning up out of the blue, deals were falling in to place without effort, and all my desires began to manifest.

Whatever you think of this secret, you must put it into practice. It's not your job to think about it, or judge it, or work out whether it's your kind of thing. Your job is to use the ultimate secret power, which is known as The One Process.

The secret power they told me about had nothing to do with talent or effort or networking. There were no business secrets. The power they told me about can be unlocked with a simple mental trick. When you know this secret, it completely changes your luck, your life and your ability to manifest the things you deserve.

Within days, the desires I'd spent decades trying to acquire fell into my life, without effort.

As I said, I've reads hundreds of books on this subject, and not once did I see a book that contained the secret power of The One Process.

Will It Really Work?

I am sure that when you've read the whole book you will be very excited, because it will all make sense. You'll get a feeling for how quickly this can work for you.

But there is a danger that three months from now you'll realize nothing much has changed in your life. If that's the case, it means you read the book but didn't act on it. You must apply the technique. It's easy to apply. It doesn't even take faith or belief. Just try the technique. It takes only a few moments each day.

But I need you to make a promise to yourself, right now, that you will try the technique no matter how simple it seems. If you don't, I guarantee that nothing will happen. If you do, I guarantee that your life will change.

The One Process genuinely has the power to attract your desires into your life, and takes so little time to perform, but it will not work if you read the book without doing the technique. So, every day, do the technique and watch the results.

As soon as you've read this book, you can apply the technique and immediately see changes take place in your life.

Don't waste too much your time trying to work out how or why this power works. I don't know how or why it works. But it works, so I use the power. I feel the same way about cars – when I get in one, there's a lot of mysterious engineering and chemistry going on. It interests me, it baffles me, but I don't let it stop me driving. I get in the car and hit the gas.

You're lucky enough to have access to this secret, so use the gift you now have. It's that simple. Once it's working well for you, feel free to come up with theories and explanations, but never let them get in the way of actually applying this power in your life.

There is nothing more important than putting The One Process into practice, to harness the power that's available to you.

It really does feel as though you get the Universe on your side, so you feel life's working for you, rather than against you.

Does It Work For Everything?

I don't want to exaggerate what this technique can do for you. It can't make your life completely free of danger, accidents and drama. Accidents happen, and life is a dangerous adventure at times. This power will not protect you from all harm.

There are many books out there that promise to cure your diseases and save you from all harm. To be honest, I don't think that's possible. Look at all the rich, famous and successful people you know. They still have problems, and eventually they die. The same will be true for you. After reading this book you will still have problems, and eventually you will die. But on the way to the end of this life, you will have a wonderful time.

Using The One Process you can certainly reduce the chaos in your life. When things do go wrong, you'll be better equipped than most people to find rapid solutions. You'll be able to attract the solutions you need.

This book gives you a secret weapon to use in any time of distress. Whatever happens, whatever goes wrong or surprises you, you will have the power to find the best solution in the fastest possible time.

And when things are going well, you can choose to create the life you want, rather than having your life happen to you.

The technique I'm revealing to you is called The One Process because there is just one, simple process that you need to apply in your daily life.

Few people know of this power, but it is the absolute key to attracting what you want.

When Power Comes Easily

You'll be relieved to know that this book is easy to understand. The technique that unlocks this power can be applied in moments. Quite simply, it lets you make things happen the way you want them to happen. You do not need to spend hours meditating or visualizing. The real secret is that it's incredibly easy.

The One Process is not well known. It is not like other so-called success techniques, and until now, it has been kept very secret.

I have to admit, that when I first heard about *The Secret* movie, I wondered if they were going to reveal The One Process. I could tell from the first trailers that there were going to be references to The Law of Attraction, but what if they revealed The One Process? Was my deepest secret really about to be revealed to the world?

When I finally saw *The Secret* movie (long before I read the book) I was amazed that all it did was reveal a very basic overview of The Law of Attraction. I knew it would be popular, and it was, because it gave people hope.

But a few years later, there are millions of people trying to refine Law of Attraction techniques, reading countless books, and going to endless seminars, and even going on cruises to find out more. If it really works, does there really need to be such a circus going on around it all?

I can promise you that you don't need to spend too much time on The Law of Attraction. It contains some useful truths, and some indications of how to live your life. But all you really need is The One Process.

Just The Facts

I want to keep this book as short and simple as possible. I want these ideas to be so simple that you have instant access to them. This is meant to be easy. So I'm not going to pad out the book with endless theories and ideas.

There are many courses for sale on the Internet, that give you hours and hours of recordings and endless books and bonus reports. And do you know why? They do that to make you feel like you've bought something worth $100 or $400. I don't want to trick you like that.

I want you to use the book and find that it works. So, when you start using The One Process, one of the first things you should do is attract some extra money – the same amount you paid for the book. That's far more useful to you – and me – than giving you a whole load of 'bonus' materials that will simply waste your time.

So I will not bore you with case histories or stories of personal success. Most success books tell great success stories, to get you in the mood. These stories, whether true or not, can help a reader to believe in any given technique or principle. But in reality, I can't convince you of anything. Only you will know if this technique works.

If you're feeling skeptical, fifty convincing stories won't convince you of anything. It makes much more sense to give you the technique, and compel you to use it as soon as possible. (I do have lots of amazing stories to tell, but I'd rather you created your own. Follow the principles, and you won't need convincing by other peoples' stories.)

So, putting all stories aside, I'm just going to give you the facts. I'll tell you exactly what to do, and then you must do it. I will explain a simple technique and you must apply it.

To prove that it works, one of your first tasks should be to attract some money, out of the blue, that will cover the cost of this book.

That is a very easy thing to achieve with The One Process. Try it, and when the money appears, enjoy the moment.

Understand that you can attract anything you want in this way. Now, depending on your situation, money might not be the very first thing you attract. Some people find it better to start with even smaller things, and build up gradually. More on that later. But rest assured, we'll soon get money turning up in your life, out of the blue.

You may, of course, have your doubts about all this. It's OK to be skeptical. It's absolutely fine to have major doubts. You don't need to believe in this power to make it work. But you do need to apply the technique. Be as skeptical as you want, but apply the technique every day and see what happens.

The only thing that can prevent you from being successful is laziness. If you're too lazy to apply The One Process, you'll never know its power.

If you wonder why I'm repeating this point, it's because I don't want you to waste this opportunity. Imagine if Aladdin was given the lamp and never bothered to use it?

You are being given something precious. Use it. Keep using it until you get so good at using it that it becomes second nature.

But be patient. Don't be desperate for instant change. Desperation pushes results away.

Sometimes, results come instantly. Often they take much longer. Your job is not to force things to change, but to use this technique, then get on with your life.

If the changes happen instantly, that's great. If not, don't worry. When you use this power, everything happens exactly when it's meant to, so there is never any need for impatience.

You Don't Need To Believe

Of course, I can't expect you to believe what I'm saying without any evidence. You'll get evidence soon enough, but in the meantime; you can pretend that you believe. You can pretend that you have faith. You can act as though the technique works. If you do that, it will work.

Here is one of the greatest secrets in the Universe: the Universe doesn't care whether you genuinely believe something or not. All that matters is that you act as though you believe.

And the way you 'act as though' is by practicing The One Process every day.

Many great actors, writers and business people have said that they became experts by pretending to be good until they were good.

So I don't expect you to believe in the power I describe, but starting from this moment, you can pretend that you do, you can pretend that it will work. You can pretend that it's going to make huge changes in your life. And the Universe will respond as though you genuinely believe.

The best way to pretend is to act as though you believe. So do the technique, every day.

That's all there is to it. It only takes a couple of minutes.

The Secret of All Success

When I bought my first self-help book, I felt slightly embarrassed. This book claimed to hold the secrets to wealth and success, but I found it difficult to believe.

How could a book teach anybody success? Why would a truly successful person bother to write a success book? I read the book, and then I bought some more, and read every approach to self-improvement and success that I could get my hands on.

I read ancient texts and modern ideas. What struck me, after a short while, is that they all said the same thing. This is pretty much what Rhonda Byrne discovered when she did her research for *The Secret*. The truth is that there is no secret in *The Secret*– there are a few principles that have been around for a long time, and all successful people use them to some degree.

These principles are nothing to do with working hard, thinking laterally or better management. These principles are all about changing your thoughts, to affect your reality.

Every book I ever read on success said the same thing. Your thoughts become things. What you think about appears in your life. It made sense, on some level, but I still struggled to find success.

I kept reading those books, and kept trying to use the principles. Over the years, the books got better, the techniques were refined, and it became easy to see that there were six core principles, that just about everybody agreed upon.

Corporate managers, visionaries, great leaders and the finest artists have used these principles. They can be revealed in a few lines, and are so simple it's easy to dismiss them as nonsense.

And there is, of course, the secret of The One Process. This brings the power of the other principles to life. And very few people know about it.

The first six principles are listed below. These are nothing new. You can read them all over the internet, free. I'm not offering you inside information here. It's probably very familiar to you. But even so, it's good stuff.

If you just glance through them, you might think they sound far-fetched, too simplistic, over-familiar or plain old baloney. That's OK. What's important is that you get to grips with this material. No matter how simple it seems, it's incredibly powerful, and you'll need to use it in your life.

Even if you've read every book there is on The Law of Attraction, please read what follows, because it will help you to get so much more out of The One Process.

But please note *this is just a recap of everything that has gone before.*

What you see below is *not* The One Process. This is just a summary of other techniques. The One Process will follow, shortly.

The Law of Attraction is not the whole story, but it does contain some truth. It's worth using what's good from The Law of Attraction.

So, what follows is a summary of all the success techniques in the world. Once you know these, you can move on to The One Process.

When summarized, the main success theories in the world come down to this these six principles.

Principle 1: Decide what you really, really want.

Principle 2: Imagine that what you want has already happened.

Principle 3: Feel grateful, as though your desire has already manifested.

Principle 4. Be patient and allow your desire (or something better) to occur. This is also known as "letting go".

Principle 5. Feel gratitude when your result manifests.

Principle 6: Feel gratitude generally.

And that's it. That's all you will ever get from most books and courses. And it's actually pretty good.

You can read hundreds of success books or join countless self-development courses, or go to endless workshops and whatever angles they come at it from, these are the essential secret of all success.

You may be familiar with the concept already. It's been used by just about everybody who was ever successful. I am not going to argue with this. It is correct. You've just read the equivalent of $30,000 worth of success books.

The problem is, those six principles can be difficult to understand, difficult to live, and they don't always work as well as you want them to work.

But don't worry; we have something much more exciting to add to the mix.

The Pattern of Success

Even though I'm going to let you in on a much greater secret, never underestimate the power of the above wisdom. It can take you a long way.

If this summary seems ridiculous, or over simplistic, you can buy those books, and read about the millions of successful people who use these exact principles. But, to be honest, you're better off just trying The One Process and seeing what happens. You'll be amazed at the results.

In the following days and weeks, listen carefully to interviews with truly successful people, and you'll see them allude to these principles. They may never say outright, 'This is my secret to success,' but you will hear the spirit of these principles echoed over and over again by the successful, the famous and the wealthy.

These principles work. But as I say, despite their apparent simplicity, most people find them difficult to use. Why?

Well, people aren't always sure what they really want, they have trouble thinking about possible futures, they can't generate gratitude out of thin air, and they are never patient. People hate visualizing and they hate waiting. Letting go of your desire is just about impossible.

This is why The Law of Attraction fails so often.

So, although these instructions for success are correct, they are difficult to apply to your life, and the result is that for many people, they don't work.

It's like telling an overweight person to Eat Less and Move About More. It's essentially correct, but you only need to look at the billion-dollar diet industry to know that people need more than this.

When it comes to success and The Law of Attraction, writers and gurus try to clarify those six principles, but often they make you spend hours meditating or visualizing or chanting affirmations. Which is why most people give up.

Let's face it, the truly rich, famous and successful do not lie around visualizing all day.

That's a very important point that you should think about.

Do you know many successful people?

If so, you'll know that they spend most of their lives working at what they love, and the rest of the time living a great and exciting life.

They do not spend a lot of time practicing 'success techniques'. They do what they love and live life to the full.

How To Stay Successful

Doing what you love, of course, pretty much takes care of the above six principles. At least, it does once you're successful.

I have found that successful people are so relaxed about being successful that they find it easy to picture their desires, and they just assume their desires will come to pass. And so the successful remain successful.

For people 'trying' to be successful it's another matter. No matter how hard you meditate or visualize, or try to let go, it's difficult to stop yourself from feeling a sense of struggle.

If you ever hang around successful people, or - even better- famous people, then you'll get a feel for the power they hold. Their presence and their self-belief keeps the money and good times flowing.

I'm the first to admit that it's not easy to get yourself into that frame of mind. But don't worry. The secret contained within this book gives you the power to attract what you want, even if you find the other six principles difficult to master.

Which means that as you get more of what you want and solve all your problems, and attract all your dreams, you'll be able to live those six principles automatically, without worrying about them.

A thousand dollars in your wallet is worth more than a year of visualization and meditation.

This is the exact opposite of what all The Law of Attraction gurus will tell you. They will tell you to feel rich first, and 'get into the vortex' or some other weird phrase – in other words, they insist that you should feel perfectly happy and successful even when you're not. Only then, they say, can you be rich. I'm here to tell you that they are wrong.

I have seen The One Process put money in pockets, and bring success out of the blue.

The Power of Results

When you've got 1000 dollars in your pocket, which you can spend freely, there's no need to visualize yourself as rich, or feel as though you're rich, because you'll already feel rich. This book can put 1000 dollars in your pocket. And it can give you so much more.

My advice is to use the deeper secret of this book – The One Process - to get some of the stuff you want, so you can start to feel richer and more confident about success. You'll then start to feel rich and successful, and you'll then continue to attract riches and success.

Inspiration isn't as useful as a handful of stuff. So, use The One Process to get more money, more success, and then keep your eye on the other six principles.

I'm not criticizing the standard Law of Attraction material for the sake of being contrary – it's worked well for me in the past. But I've heard from so many people who love listening to and reading the material, but find it doesn't actually work for them in the real world.

It's all very well to be told, 'Feel good thoughts and be patient,' but people find it difficult to be patient.

Beyond Positive Thinking

With The One Process you need less patience than usual. Things will change quickly. Of course, sometimes patience is the absolute key to success, but at other times, you can be assured that results will come in days or even hours.

With traditional Law of Attraction you're told to 'let go', and not worry about whether or not your desire will come to pass. But most people think, 'It would be a lot easier to stop worrying about paying the bills, if I had the money to pay the bill.' In other words, life becomes much easier when you actually get the stuff you want.

Patience is a vital skill. But the good news is that when you use The One Process, you don't need quite as much patience. You don't need to let go of your desire.

Again, this is the exact opposite of what most Law of Attraction gurus say. They will tell you to stop thinking about your desires, as though any doubts you have might frighten your success away. It doesn't work like that. You don't have to let go of your desire or get into a perfect state of mind. You can be cranky and depressed and uptight and still get what you're looking for.

This is good news.

Using The One Process you can get money, win things, meet the people you want to meet- anything. It gives you the immediate physical feedback you want. That's not to say you can be impatient and frivolous with this power, but if you want money, a car, a new house, The One Process works faster and more effectively than anything else around.

When you master The One Process, you need to keep the other six principles in place, as part of your life, which is why they are presented here in this clear, simple form. When you combine these six principles with the incredibly simple One Process technique, the results will be far more impressive, and faster than you ever dreamed possible.

The One Process

If you've skipped ahead to this section to see what the Ultimate Secret is, then your wish is my command. The secret of The One Process is this: any feeling will do, so long as it's intense.

This single line makes absolutely no sense when taken out of context, so you really need to read the whole book. If you skipped ahead, please read the whole book, then come back here.

For those of you who've actually read the whole book up to this point, and started putting the other principles into practice, here we go.

As mentioned earlier, people find it very difficult to visualize the future and feel positive feelings. Every book ever written about success or Law of Attraction will tell you that you have to visualize with a genuine feeling of appreciation, expectation and excitement, free of all doubt and skepticism.

Easier said than done.

But the good news is: *any feeling will do*. When you imagine your future, it doesn't matter what you feel, so long as you feel *something* intensely.

Not many people know this.

Those who do know this fact are able to manifest the most outrageous desires in the fastest possible time.

Don't underestimate this secret. It makes things happen, just as you desire.

I can tell you in all honesty that I went from virtual poverty, to having a multi-million dollar deal in my industry, in less than a year. I used The One Process. It works.

You should note, however, that it took me almost a year. I didn't try to land the deal on the first day. I didn't try to win the lottery. Instead, I attracted many smaller miracles to help me on my way to that deal. This is where you must learn to be skillful.

Learn to attract the next important goal, rather than the final goal.

Learn what it is that you really need to achieve next, rather than what you need to achieve next year.

If you're hungry, manifest a meal. If you're in debt, manifest money to pay off your debts. Then work on being a millionaire.

Don't Limit Your Dreams

I'm not telling you to limit your dreams, but that you need to work in stages. You can work absolute miracles with this technique, but you need to be clever. Attract what you need to help you on your journey. If you do, it will work, every time.

The One Process is the process of thinking about your desire, and applying an intense emotion. Any emotion.

Here's an example. You want a new car. You really want a new car. But every time you imagine the car, you can't help feeling worried about the cost. Even when you try to feel good about owning the car, and picture yourself being happy, it all feels a bit fake and unenthusiastic.

No matter how hard you visualize, you worry about how much it would cost, or how you could ever be the sort of person who drives that car. As a result, you push it further away from your life. Your visualization actually makes it less likely that you'll get that car. The standard techniques, taught in all success books, actually make it harder to get what you want. And most people find it difficult to visualize anything, so the whole process feels forced.

Here's The One Process approach:

You think about the car. You don't have to visualize it. Just think about it, think about why you want it. At the same time, *you think about something else that makes you feel good* – perhaps a day out with your best friend. Do that, and the car will be yours, sooner than you thought possible? Don't worry about how it will come to you. Don't try to work out how this can happen. Just watch it happen.

Any Feeling Will Do

Every success book I've read says you should picture the desired result, and feel good about it, feel gratitude for it. But that's not true. The secret of The One Process is that you merely need to think about your desire, and feel something else strongly, and the desire will come to pass.

It's as though emotion is fuel.

Think about your desire, and feel something intensely, and your desire will become real.

Can it really be this simple?

Yes. I'll give you more detail, to make sure you get the most out of this, but this is the essential secret. Think about your desire, and feel something intensely. It will then come into your life. I don't know why this works, but it does.

Please don't dismiss this idea, if it seems too simple.

Be grateful for the fact that it is so simple.

Everybody else will tell you to visualize perfectly, meditate powerfully and to clear your mind of desire. That's a lot of hard work. This technique is so simple it sounds impossible. But that's why it's the best technique in the universe. It takes just a few minutes, each day.

Can you use bad feelings as well as good? To be perfectly honest, you can, but be aware that passive feelings such as boredom and depression don't appear to work as well. More active feelings, such as anger or hate seem to work well. But be warned, every time you carry out this technique, you tend to attract more of that feeling. As well as getting your desire, you get more of the emotion you used. So, if you use anger or hate, you may end up feeling more anger or hate in your life.

So, to keep it simple, and use good, positive feelings. Use feelings of elation and happiness.

Unlocking The One Process

How do you generate feelings out of thin air? Simple. You use your memory.

When you remember something clearly, you automatically re-experience the original emotion.

Remember any time when you won something, or something went right, or something felt fantastic or loving.

The amazing thing about memory is that when you remember a feeling, you feel it all over again.

This is your secret weapon.

Use your memories to order up good feelings, and use them to power your desires.

Here's an example. This shows you step by step how to use this technique.

Recently, I wrote a book (under a pseudonym), and my publisher wanted me to get quotes from various people, to plaster all over the book. I didn't want to do this. It was too difficult, it was too time consuming. Every time I thought about this, it made me angry and impatient.

So, I followed the six principles and applied The One Process.

Firstly, I decide what I really wanted. I wanted the quotes to flow in effortlessly without any effort from me.

Secondly, I imagined the quotes coming in and I imagined how good that would feel.

This took me automatically to principle three. I imagine what it would feel like if my dream came true. Phew – big sigh of relief.

This is all very simple. It took less than ten seconds.

Then I applied The One Process.

First of all, I searched for a potent emotion. I am a fan of motor sports, and my favorite Formula One driver is Lewis Hamilton. I had recently stayed up late watching Lewis drive to a glorious victory. The emotions of that race had me jumping up and down for days. So, there was my source of intense emotion.

What did I want? Quotes for my book. So I thought about the quotes coming in. I thought about my email box filling with them. And before I could start worrying about the hows and the whys, I remembered the race that Lewis won, and felt my excitement and joy. Then I pictured the quotes coming in again, and straight away went back to my memory of Lewis. Simple. It took less than two minutes.

It takes some practice, but you will soon learn to hold two things in your mind. Your desire, and your potent memory. When you think about them both, they mingle, and that is magic.

When you perform this process, after a certain time you know that it's 'got through'. You just feel when you've done enough. It feels as though a switch has been clicked. As soon as that happens, stop, confidently knowing you've done enough. It usually takes less than two minutes. TWO MINUTES to attract whatever you want.

For the next two weeks my email box was filled with the quotes I needed. My publisher had organized everything for me. That's nothing short of a miracle.

Every time this happens I feel a little whoosh of excitement that borders on disbelief, and then I feel, 'Yes, of course, this thing works.' It's very important that you let that second feeling linger, rather than testing The One Process over and over again. Feel tremendous appreciation and gratitude for what this power can bring you.

Working With Universal Powers

Don't worry that you are somehow tricking the Universe, or cheating. From what I've seen, the Universe answers our requests, whatever they may be, so long as they are made clearly.

We make our requests with our thoughts and images, and we give them power by feeling intensely.

And, amazingly, it doesn't matter where those feelings come from.

The Universe doesn't seem to be interested in our desires and hopes – but it lets us order exactly what we want so long as we speak the language that the universe uses. Images and feelings.

The Law of Attraction is real and it works, but it fails for people so frequently for one very simple reason. When you picture what you don't have (car, holiday, new job), the image is so emotionally charged that it's difficult to generate genuine feelings of excitement and appreciation. When you picture that car you can't help but feel some degree of poverty. After all, the reason you don't have that new car is that you can't afford it.

If you're feeling lonely, and picture yourself with lots of friends, you'll still probably feel quite lonely – and thus attract more loneliness.

When you think about what you don't have, there's the risk that you'll drum up these feelings of lack. This is where The One Process can save you.

Picture the future you desire, use your memory to create a good feeling, and while that feeling lingers, picture your desire again.

How often do you do this? Every day. It takes about two minutes for each desire. If you're wise you'll work on just a few desires at a time.

Making Money

Let's say you've just bought this book. I bet I can guess what your number one desire is. Usually, it's more money. Fine, you need more money. Be specific. How much do you need, right now. How much do you want right now?

If you're currently on a low income, with lots of bills and no real sources of income, don't try to create a million dollars. It might happen, but it probably won't.

The best way get to a million dollars is in stages. Find an extra $100 this week. An extra $20,000 over six months. An extra $500,000 next year.

In other words, what amount of money would have a positive benefit, without turning your life upside down? If you're currently on a very low income and actually received a million dollars, I am certain a million dollars would wreck your life. You can be a millionaire, but don't try to get there in a week. Instead, let it build. Get there in a year or two.

This is not to say that I'm being traditionally realistic. Far from it. To be realistic, in everyday terms, would be to say you'll always earn the same amount, and nothing will ever change. Using The One Process you can make miracles happen. But what is a miracle to you? If you earn $60,000 a year, a miracle might be $10,000 out of the blue. But if you're on a very low income, a miracle might be an extra $200. If you're a millionaire, a miracle might be another $5,000,000.

Look for your own miracles.

If you're starting from a very poor position, you will get rich, but let it happen gradually.

On the other hand, don't think, 'Well, I've never had more than $50 spare, so I'll wish for $50.' Ask yourself what amount of money would really help you get through this next week. Be honest. You'll know whether you're being honest with yourself by how you feel. If it feels ridiculously impossible, don't go there. If it feels mostly impossible, but just a bit exciting, that's the perfect goal to aim for.

Once you know the figure, you can get that figure, and a little more besides. If you're a struggling actor, don't try to land a role in an A-list movie. Use The One Process to get a good role in a small movie. You'll get to the big movie eventually.

If you want to be a great novelist, don't use the technique to get a million dollar deal. Use it to get your first deal, or to sell a short story.

Most success techniques fail because they promise miracles that you don't believe are possible. The beautiful thing about The One Process is that it can give you things that are just outside your range of belief. It will keep surpassing you.

So, let's say you want to drive a Ferrari but you're poor, and don't own a car at all. Should you use The One Process to attract a Ferrari? No. Use it to attract a good car. A car better than you ever thought you could own. Get that car first. Then aim for the Ferrari.

Two Important Questions

The best way to use The One Process is this: Ask yourself two questions.

What do I expect?

What is my impossible dream?

Then find something in between the two answers. Aim for that, and you will get it, every time.

So, let's say you want that Ferrari. What do you expect? Truthfully, you expect you won't get any car, because you can't afford a new car. And your crazy dream is to have a Ferrari. What lies somewhere in between? A brand new car, better than any you've driven before. Use The One Process to attract that. Once it appears in your life, use The One Process to attract an even better car, and gradually work up to the Ferrari.

I have used this technique many times, and it only fails when I aim for things that are too far outside my current world. If, for instance, I used The One Process to attract my own airplane, it probably wouldn't work. Why? Because I don't really love flying. Because I've never tried to get a pilot's license. It's not really a dream for me.

If I suddenly found that my dream was to fly, then I'd use The One Process to get a pilot's license. And then a plane.

The One Process works, so put it into practice. Use it to get the things you want now.

What to think about?

When you 'think about your desire' what should you actually think?

Some people can visualize in perfect 3D, like a full color movie. If you can do that, go ahead. Most people can't, but that's Ok. Just think about why it would be good to achieve your goal.

So, let's say you're trying to manifest a brand new car. Think about how excited you'd be to drive it away, think about the pleasure you'd get from showing it to a friend. Think about anything that genuinely appeals to you about this desire. Just mull it over in your mind.

And at the same time, think about a memory that's full of intense emotion.

It's that simple

Don't make it more complicated than this. If you're no good at visualizing, it really doesn't matter. You still have enough imagination to work this magic.

More On The Six Principles

As clearly and precisely as possible, I'm going to look at the six principles for success. I'm going to distil all my knowledge from thousands of books and hundreds of experts, and give you a precise, simple explanation of each. I'll show you the standard pitfalls and the very best solutions.

When The One Process is working, you'll want to apply these principles as well.

If you're wise – and I sincerely hope that you are –you will try to put these principles into practice *now*. They will make life much easier, and you'll probably have to use The One Process less frequently if you put these principles into practice.

Principle 1: Decide what you really, really want.

When you know you can have anything, you will find that you focus in on what you really want.

You may find that some of the things you thought you wanted aren't that special after all.

Accept that you can attract anything and any situation. Spend some time thinking about what you really want.

In effect, imagine that you've been granted 100 wishes. What would you actually wish for?

Before you go any further, it's worth taking time to work this out. If you're already very clear on this, great, let's move on. If not, then everybody who's ever been successful would say to you, stop and think and search your feelings, and find out what you really want. And write it down.

Don't fall into the trap of saying, 'I want to earn millions and have a mansion with a TV in every room.' That *might* be what you want, but it probably isn't. You'd probably hate that lonely mansion after a while.

I knew one man who thought he wanted that kind of place to live, but once he had access to The One Process, he realized that what he really wanted to do was write comedy for television. And now he does. He's not the richest man I know, but he's one of the happiest.

Principle 2: Imagine that what you want has already happened.

This is usually called 'visualization'. The basic idea is that you picture your desire in great detail. Most people find it difficult to create clear images. That doesn't matter.

Just thinking about your desire is enough.

Think about your desire and why you desire it. A good game to play is The Because Game. Let's imagine you want to get a new car. You would write, 'I want a new car because….' And then list all the reasons you want a new car.

It is vital that you are honest. Don't think the Universe is going to judge you if you write, 'I want a new car because it will impress my brother. Because I hate the junk heap I'm driving now.'

If your thoughts and feelings are petty or negative, so be it. Let them out, write them down, feel them.

Principle 3: Feel grateful, as though your desire has already manifested.

This is just a case of pretending, for a moment, that your desire has come to pass.

So, let's say you want a new car. You've written your reasons in your Because List. At the end, write something like, 'I now have my new car and it feels great.'

This is simply a case of imagining what it would be like to have your dream come true.

There are hundreds of books that complicate this subject beyond belief, but it is very simple. When you picture your desire, picture it as a memory, as though it has already happened. Remember how good it felt when that dream came true.

If you ever find yourself worrying about whether a desire will manifest, remember it happening and how good you felt. This little mental trick works extremely well.

For a moment, just imagine what it would be like if your dream came true, and if you like, write that feeling down.

Principle 4. Be patient and allow your desire (or something better) to occur. This is also known as "letting go".

Again, thousands of books have been written on 'letting go', and they tend to make it more complicated than it needs to be.

It is true that if you visualize something strongly and then stop thinking about it, that dream will come true in super-fast time.

It is also true that if you visualize something strongly and then worry about whether or not it will come true, or how it will come true, then the entire operation is probably wasted.

But letting go is a paradox. If you want something, are you really expected to forget about it for a while?

Let's imagine you want a new car because your old one is just about broken, and you want to impress your brother, and you just *love* new cars. OK, you've imagined this. You've felt it as though it's inevitable. And now you're supposed to forget about it? Really?

On the one hand, these principles say we should desire strongly, but then they say we should forget our desire? This sounds crazy.

In truth, it's all about confidence. If you really feel that something is inevitable, you don't spend time worrying about whether it will happen or why it will happen.

For most people, you absolutely know that you will get to eat dinner tonight, so you don't spend any time worrying about that. You have 'let go' automatically. You never spend time visualizing dinner and letting go of your desire, because you know dinner will happen. You need the same level of confidence when it comes to other manifestations.

The sad and simple truth is that there are millions of people out there visualizing and pretending to let go, but they still worry about the money, the difficulty, the impossibility.

In practice, most people can't let go, because the desire is too intense. You wouldn't have bought this book if you didn't have intense desires, so how are you supposed to let go of them?

There is a cure. Let's say you're trying to get a really good car. It's out of your usual price range. A bit sporty. Something special. Fine. You go through principles 1, 2 and 3. You play The Because Game. You use The One Process to attract the car. Now, you're meant to forget about it. But you won't be able to.

So, rather than trying to avoid thinking about it, every time you remember the car, just think how good it would be to have the car. This is the simplest solution in the world, but it works.

You can take this a step further, if you want to, by pretending a memory. So instead of thinking, 'Wouldn't it be great if I did get that car,' remember getting the car and think, 'Wasn't it great when I got that car.' If you find this too difficult, stick to the simpler process of thinking how great it would be to get the car.

This simple technique is far better than trying to forget about your desires. If you find yourself worrying how to get the car, or how much it would cost, quickly remind yourself to play this game.

You can't forget your desires, so don't try to do so. The key is to avoid treating them as worries.

So, whatever you dream of, when it comes up in your thoughts, just think, 'Wouldn't it be great if that happened,' or 'Wasn't it great when that happened.'

This is far more powerful than forgetting or "letting go".

Principle 5. Feel appreciation when your result manifests

When your dreams come true, don't feel guilty. Don't worry about your power. Instead, appreciate what you've managed to attract.

If it makes you feel better to share your wealth, then do so, but do so out of joy, not guilt or obligation. The Universe wants you to be prosperous and happy, so revel in the joy you create.

Principle 6: Feel appreciation generally

There is always something bad going on in the world. If you want, you can spend your whole life worrying about war, the economy, death, disease, murder and abuse. Yes, this stuff goes on. But if you look at the balance of your day, there's a lot to appreciate. Even on a day that you might call a 'bad day', there's a lot to be happy about. Learn to see this good in your life.

All the most successful people will tell you that, no matter how wealthy you are, if you can't appreciate a sunset or the wind in your hair, you're wasting your time.

Every day, make a point of appreciating things; even if it's just the roof over your head, and the food that you eat, or the people you care about. This sounds so simple, which is why it's so often neglected, but appreciating what you have is as powerful as any of the other principles. Feel gratitude. There are lots of books written about this, and every once of them is telling the truth. Gratitude pays. It makes the moment feel better, and it attracts more of what you desire.

Put these six principles into practice all the time.

When you really want something, use The One Process.

But keep using these six principles. If you do that, you will get everything you have dreamed of having.

Start small. Manifest a bit more money. Manifest a few small dreams. Then, when you get good at this, let your dreams take flight.

You can be, do or having anything, so have fun. You'll never look back.

Questions and Answers

I shared the idea of The One Process with a few friends. I did this before I wrote the book, and then I also gave the first few copies of the book to friends and trusted relatives, to make sure everything made sense. I also sold a limited edited of the book, to make sure everything made sense to my readers.

These helpful friends and readers raised a few questions along the way.

You might find these questions, and my answers, useful.

Q: What happens if I'm desperate for change? I need money, right now, urgently.

A: Desperation can be counter-productive, but the main technique of The One Process will help with this.

Whatever else, start small. Don't try to create a new car or a lottery win at the outset. Instead, manifest a really good day out or an unexpected gift.

When you start small, you lose the sense of desperation that's ruining your life, and before you know it you're manifesting the big stuff. If you only try to manifest the big stuff, you might not get there. But if you start small, you will get to the big stuff.

One friend of mine started by trying to manifest a cup of coffee. Ten seconds later, out of the blue, her husband offered her a cup of coffee. He never does that, normally. Now, you didn't get into The One Process to get cups of coffee. But you see my point - start small, and you learn the power of this technique, and very rapidly you'll start to attract the bigger stuff.

Q: What happens if I think about my desire and get upset or worried that I can't have it? Will that drive my goal further away?

A: If you're having difficulty with the technique, generate the emotions first. Remember something so exciting that genuine, positive emotions bubble up inside you. Then start thinking about your goal.

Every second or two, go back to the emotions; you flip backwards and forwards between the memory and the desire. This way, there's no time to start worrying.

If you feel a negative emotion or thought, go back to the memory that gave you the good emotions. Or, if all else fails, just stop. You can't do any damage if you get it wrong for a few moments.

Then, start again, making sure you use a memory that creates a really powerful feeling.

Q: Can The One Process break bad habits? Even really bad habits?

A: Yes, it can work for bad habits. But, one thing about bad habits is that they tend to come back. In other words, if you make some progress, and then revert to your old ways, don't see it as failure.

Completely eradicating a bad habit takes time, and even with The One Process at your disposal, it will take discipline and effort to defeat a habit. So use the technique to defeat the habit a day at a time, or even an hour at a time, if that's what it takes.

So, let's imagine you have three hours ahead of you, and you think you might indulge in this bad habit. The end result you want is that in three hours you will be feeling good because you defeated your habit for three hours. So, generate a good feeling (using memory) then think about getting through the next three hours without indulging in the habit.

For really bad habits, you might need to use the technique to get through the next hour. When things get better, you might only need to use The One Process to get through a full week without indulging in the habit. Eventually, when the habit is truly broken, stop giving it any attention and spend your time attracting something you want instead.

Q: Do you send out your intention with emotions just once and wait? Or should you keep doing The One Process technique until your desire manifests?

A: You don't need to do this process all the time, but repetition helps. Also, it depends on the scale of the thing. If it's something very small and believable to you, once will be enough. If it's a much bigger leap in your life, then it's worth doing this every few days.

But you don't need to spend a long time on this. Really, a couple of minutes, every day is enough.

Q: I tried it for a week, and it's not working. It's meant to work fast, right?

A: First, make sure these are things you genuinely want and feel you deserve, especially when starting out.

One person I know tried to attract lots of money and all sorts of new things he wanted to own, but he just didn't believe it could happen. As a result, he was very half-hearted in his practice of The One Process.

So after a few days, I encouraged him to try with something smaller. He used The One Process to attract a good evening out, rather than the boring ones he was used to. It worked.

Then he tried to attract an enjoyable dinner with his parents (free of the usual arguments). It worked. After a few days of this, he was so confident that he moved on to money and success, and they came. It's worth starting really small, to prove to yourself that it works. But don't stay on the small things. I really dislike it when I hear people saying that The Law of Attraction helps them attract parking spaces, without any major benefits. The small manifestations are used to get you going. Move on from them.

Once you feel you've done the technique enough times - and a week is often enough - you can just stop and let the results come. *But let them come when they come.* It might take a week, it might take a month, it might even take longer. Somebody once said that infinite patience yields immediate rewards. It's one of the most difficult things to get right, but if you do the technique, and then just let the results come when they want to come, that's far better than saying, 'I want it this week.'

If you place no time limitations on your desire, the Universe can flex far more for you. If you act as though you don't care when it happens, it will probably happen much faster.

Q: Should I keep using the same memories over and over again?

A: When it comes to the memories, make sure they are intense, and that as you remember them, you actually feel the feelings again. If a memory continues to generate strong feelings for you, there's no reason to stop using it. Should a memory burn out then find another. If it doesn't actually make you feel something, it's not going to do any good.

Some people just watch comedy shows or DVDs of their favorite movies to create the strong emotions, and this is a perfectly acceptable approach. If it works, use it.

Q: I want to win the lottery, but you say 'start small'. Can't I have a big dream come true?

A: You can have a big dream come true. That's probably why you got into The One Process. But there are many reasons to start small, and many reasons to avoid trying to win the lottery.

The problem with the lottery is that it's the strongest image in our culture of outrageous luck. On some level, we all believe it's just about impossible to win the lottery.

We've all heard the phrase, 'There's about as much chance of that happening as winning the lottery.' As such, people who win the lottery tend to do so by chance. The lottery involves such an outrageous level of random chaos that attempting to control it is difficult. That's not to say that it's impossible, but it's certainly not the best way to make money.

What I would say is that your goal is far more important than how you get there. If you want to have the millions of dollars that a lottery win could bring, your job is to use The One Process technique to get that future. You don't need to worry about how it will happen.

If you enjoy games of luck such as the lottery, by all means play, but never play them if it's going to make you feel like a loser when you don't win.

It is better to improve your finances in small shifts than in huge leaps. History shows that lottery winners are so unused to managing money - because it takes quite some skill to handle that amount of money - that most of them are unhappy and lose their money.

Having millions is a great goal, but let yourself get there in any way that the Universe offers. And there is no harm in starting a bit smaller. It's better to spend a year learning to use this technique to win smaller things, than to spend five more years not winning the lottery.

So, if you like winning things, still enter the lottery, but enter other things too. Try, for the next few months, to win small prizes, and then bigger prizes, such as cars. As you get better at this, you will find a way to the lifestyle you imagine. But remember; don't worry about how you get these things. Winning things isn't the only way. Be open to any and all possibilities.

Q: OK, I've used The One Process - do I just sit back and wait for things to happen?

A: Let's imagine you want to be an actor. Do you just sit back and wait for the phone to ring, with the offer of a role in a major movie? Of course not.

Use The One Process to find a good acting coach, then start getting some good auditions. Then land a few decent roles, and keep working your way to the top.

If you do nothing but sit at home watching TV, the message you send to the Universe is that you don't really want anything.

When you do everything you can to reach your goal, joyfully and without fear, things happen very fast.

So, whether you want to meet your soulmate, earn a fortune or be famous, don't just sit back and wait. Use The One Process, but then get out there and actually do something to make a difference to your life.

Seven Secrets For Attracting A Better Life

The following secrets are more powerful than the information you find in most success books and Law of Attraction Courses.

Some of these secrets have already been revealed, earlier in the book, to some extent, but read on to enjoy the extra detail.

Keep these secrets mind as you use The One Process, and your success is assured.

Secret # 1: What's the one thing you must do to attract more money?

The wealthiest man I ever met told me something truly wonderful. I asked him what he thought was the best way to make money. He said, 'You're asking the wrong question. You should ask me what's the best way to spend money.' So I did.

And he said, 'Joyfully. Whether you're buying a sandwich or a house, spend your money with joy, or don't spend it at all.'

There is no more powerful way to attract money than to enjoy spending it. That doesn't mean you should spend more than you can afford. If you spend more than you can afford, deep down you know that you're getting into debt, and that makes you feel poor. So you attract more poverty. Don't go out and buy a Ferrari to try and make yourself feel wealthy.

But it's worth learning to enjoy the feeling of spending money, no matter how much or how little you spend.

If you can spend 25c with joy, that's a good start.

Everybody feels good when they receive money, but how many people feel good when they spend money? Many people feel some sense of guilt, regret or fear when they spend, especially when they spend large amounts, or when they feel they've spent too much on themselves. This is a mistake. You should do everything you can to enjoy the feeling of spending, every time you spend.

There is no stronger way to signal to the Universe that you appreciate having money than if you enjoy spending it. And then the Universe gives you more.

If you're running out of money, how are you supposed to spend joyfully? It takes practice, but you can always find a way. Even when you're paying bills and taxes, you can find a way to appreciate the service you're getting, or the benefits you're bringing to others.

When you spend with joy in your heart, money flows into your life faster than you can ever spend it.

Secret # 2: I've had a lot of bad luck recently. According to The Secret movie and Abraham-Hicks, it's all my fault for thinking negative thoughts. What am I doing wrong?

People have known about The Law of Attraction and similar ideas for centuries, but only in recent decades have they started to say that our thoughts are responsible for everything that happens in our lives. Can this new theory really be true? It seems insane to suggest that every accident, illness, war or misfortune was attracted by the victims. Did everybody in the World Trade Centre have so many negative thoughts that they attracted a terrorist attack? It just doesn't make sense. We live in a world of chaos and chance events. Life is random, unless we take control. If you don't create your life deliberately, you will be subject to all kinds of random events, some good, many bad.

There is no fate or destiny, only the life you choose to create.

When you use The Law of Attraction, you reduce the chaos. But if you break your leg, did you really attract that? If your car gets stolen, is it your fault for having negative thoughts? Of course not. Most Law of Attraction gurus would disagree. But don't forget that miserable people win the lottery, and good people are gunned down in the street. Negative people become millionaires, while positive people die in horrible accidents.

There is no doubt that 'thoughts are things' when you deliberately create, but it is dangerous to suggest that everything in your life is caused by your casual thoughts. Your thoughts and feelings are powerful tools, which can create, but they are not enemies to be feared.

The Law of Attraction is an amazing power that can attract the life you want, and The One Process is the best way to guide it into action. You will have fewer accidents, disasters and problems than most people. But when things do go wrong, don't blame yourself or worry that your negative thoughts attracted the problem. Focus on what you want next, and use The One Process to get it.

Secret # 3: What's the number one mistake people make when trying to manifest a new reality?

The worst thing you can do is send a request out to the Universe, and then tell the Universe *how* to grant your wish.

The Universe knows better than you do, so let it do its job.

Your goal is far more important than how you get there.

If you want to have a million dollars, your job is to use The One Process to get that future. You don't need to worry about how it will happen.

If you say, 'I want this future, and the ONLY WAY I'M WILLING TO GET IT IS BY WINNING THE LOTTERY,' you are placing huge restrictions on the Universe. If you say, 'I want this future, no matter what, and I don't care how I get there,' it can happen remarkably fast. You're giving the Universe many more options, and the Universe has a fabulous imagination. Have a strong desire for that end result, and you'll get there.

I once needed to get a new house in less than a week, but I didn't even want to go out looking for houses. I just wanted the perfect house to be handed over to me. I could have said to myself, 'The only way this will happen is if I win a house,' but that would have limited my chances.

Instead, I pictured a house coming to me easily, and then let it come in whatever way it wanted to come. A relative who had previously been mean and unfriendly gave me a house three days later.

I still find it difficult to believe, but it is absolutely true. If I had tried to win the house, it might not have happened. But I didn't really care how I got it. So, I got my new house, without searching or even paying. It's mind-blowing, but it works.

So, whatever else you do, never place your limitations on the Universe. Ask for what you want, by picturing your desire with great emotion, and then let the Universe serve up the result in whatever way it chooses.

Secret # 4: Why do most people only attract small stuff? I want to earn big money.

Although *The Secret* was a great book (and movie) for getting people enthusiastic about The Law of Attraction, it spread a story about "checks appearing in the mail." Now, as anybody who's used The Law of Attraction knows, when money starts to flow, it just flows like crazy. And checks *will* turn up out of the blue, when you least expect them.

I hear stories like this every day. But a lot of people have taken this idea too far. They think that if they imagine a wealthy future, and then sit around waiting for success, it will come. Sorry, it won't. You need to get up and do something - something that excites you - to attract money. When you do what you love, the money will follow. But if you do nothing, don't expect too much in return.

The Universe rewards enthusiasm. When you live your life enthusiastically, money turns up out of the blue.

So, if you want to be an singer, get out there and start singing. If you want to find your soulmate, get out there and start meeting people.

If the only thing you want is money, think again. Imagine having a huge amount of money, and ask yourself what you would spend it on. The answer you come up with is your true desire. You don't want the money, you want what you would spend it on. You want the feeling that spending would give you. So forget the money, and think about the things you would spend the money on. When you do that, the money will come.

Secret # 5: What tiny change can make all the difference to your success with The One Process?

Let things happen when they happen. The truth is, when you go to the trouble of using The One Process, it's because you really want something. You want it badly. You want it fast. So why should you be patient?

There are two reasons. Firstly, the more patient you are, the faster things are attracted. I know that's strange, but it's absolutely true. Secondly, when you are patient, you show the Universe that you trust this process. It's the very best way to show that you have faith that the process will work.

So, even if you have doubts or fears about whether The Law of Attraction works, being patient is the best way to make things happen fast. The simplest way to do this is to avoid time-limits in the first place. Instead of saying, 'I want a new car in time for my birthday,' say to yourself, 'I want a new car.' It's the desire that's important, not the timing. Placing a time-limit on your desire simply shows the Universe that you're afraid you might not get a new car.

When you know you desire is coming, there's no need to worry about when.

So whenever you think about a desire, just remind yourself that it's coming, and that it will come at absolutely the right time. Even if you don't believe this, pretend that you do. Pretending is just as powerful as believing.

Secret # 6: Why do some people find that The Law of Attraction just doesn't work?

To achieve success with The Law of Attraction, you do this: find out what you want, picture it clearly (with feeling), and then know that it will come. If you can make yourself feel like you already have a new car, or feel like you've already met your soulmate - you will. But most people can't conjure up feelings out of thin air.

Here's what usually happens. You read about The Law of Attraction, and you decide you want to meet your soulmate, get more money, and find your dream house. So, to attract your soulmate you picture being with the person of your dreams.

But no matter how you try, you feel alone. You feel that the person is missing. And you begin to attract more loneliness. The same happens with money. You try to picture yourself being rich, but it reminds you of what's missing in your life, and you think about all your debts. No matter how you try to feel wealthy, you actually feel poor.

What's the solution? Take small steps. If you're poor, don't try to generate great wealth straight away. Try to generate a little more money. Don't try to be a millionaire next week.

All the hype about The Law of Attraction makes you think you can have anything you want, including being a millionaire. And that you can have it fast. This is true. But you can't have it instantly. In fact, if you did if it instantly, it would probably ruin your life.

So let the wealth build over a few months or years. You'll have more fun that way. It is better to do things in stages and get exactly what you want, than to spend five years getting it wrong and making things worse.

It's important to have fun along the way, and every time you manifest something - no matter how small - you know that the Universe is on your side, ready to help you out with anything you want to be, do or have.

You will be patient when required. You'll find that the more patient you are, the faster things happen. Everything you want will fall into place with remarkable ease and speed.

Secret # 7: I've heard that we should give lots of our money away, to receive more money. Is it true?

If you feel uncomfortable giving money away, don't. However, you will find that as you make more money, you want to give it away. You'll want to share, you'll want to help others. For many, this is the real joy of being rich. It becomes incredibly easy to help others, and you get an enormous buzz out of it.

But, despite what some people will tell you, there is no Universal law that says you must give away money to make money. The One Process will still work if you keep every cent for yourself. But I bet you don't.

And the truth is, many people find that giving money away, joyfully, is even more powerful than spending joyfully.

If you live like a generous person - knowing that money flows back into your life as fast as you give it away - that money will keep turning up.

One of the best tricks is to leave some money in a random place, with a note attached saying, 'Here's your money gift. Enjoy it.' Leave it on a park bench, or any other place where nobody will notice. This is so much fun, because you picture somebody finding that gift and enjoying it. Never, ever stay to watch who finds your gift. Put the money down with your note, leave, enjoy the moment and as you walk away you must claim that the money comes back to you. Say to yourself, 'Thank you, Universe, for the money that will now come back to me 100-fold.' So if you left a dollar, you'll get $100. If you left $5, you'll get $500. It doesn't cost much to play this game and it works well that I still do it often.

Most gurus say that when you give money away it should be done selflessly, but trust me, when you give joyfully, you should immediately ask that the Universe multiplies your money. It only costs $1 to try this, so give it a go, at least a few times. It is absolutely essential that you do this in secret, though, so never let people see you leaving these gifts, and never watch to see who finds them. It's far more fun to imagine somebody finding the money, so enjoy that feeling. Sharing your money was fun, and that in itself attracts more money to you.

Getting Results

You must practice The One Process to get results.

If you do nothing, nothing will happen.

Please, take a couple of minutes a day, and manifest the life you've always dreamed of having.

Michael Ellington

Printed in Great Britain
by Amazon